DISGUSTING & DREADFUL SCIENCE

Electric Shocks

and other energy evils

by Anna Claybourne

Crabtree Publishing Company

www.crabtreebooks.com

Crabtree Publishing Company
www.crabtreebooks.com
1-800-387-7650

Published in Canada
Crabtree Publishing
616 Welland Avenue
St. Catharines, ON
L2M 5V6

Published in the USA
Crabtree Publishing
PMB 59051
350 Fifth Ave, 59th Floor
New York, NY 10118

Printed in Canada/102013/MA20130906

Author: Anna Claybourne
Editorial director: Kathy Middleton
Editors: Nicola Edwards, Adrianna Morganelli
Proofreader: Crystal Sikkens
Designer: Elaine Wilkinson
Picture Researcher: Clive Gifford
Production coordinator and
   Prepress technician: Margaret Salter
Print coordinator: Katherine Berti

Published by Crabtree Publishing in 2013

First published in 2013 by Franklin Watts
Copyright © Franklin Watts 2013

Picture acknowledgements:
Corbis: 7b (Christopher Morris); 15b (Christinne Muschi/
Reuters). fotolia: 5cl (bluedarkat); 25cl (Rob Byron). iStockphoto.
com: title page (Dean Murray); eyeball cartoon (Elaine Barker);
9tl (ericsphotography); 18br (Josh Blake); 28l (karelnoppe);
back cover left (SunforRise). NASA: 25br (Bill Ingalls). National
Science Foundation: 9tr (Deven Stross). Otis Historical Archives/
National Museum of Health and Medicine: 24tr. Science Photo
Library: 9bl (National Physical Laboratory © Crown Copyright); 17t
(Peter Menzel); 19tr; 22l (Springer Medizin); 27b (Steve Munsinger).
Shutterstock.com: cover br (Cameramannz); 4b & cover (Purrush);
6b (Andrea Crisante); 6t & cover (Marynchnko Olksandr); 7tr
(Don Purcell); 8t (Semisatch); 7bl (Ivaschenko Roman); 7br (Joerg
Beuge); 9br (pzAke); 10t (koya979); 10l (AlexanderZam); 10b
(TranceDrummer); 11bl (Wong Yu Liang & Nikola Sapsenoski);
11br (Serg64); 12tr (Sarunyu_foto); 13t (Tatiana Popova); 13r
(anaken2012); 14cr (Purrush); 14cl & back cover (Aaron Amat); 15tr
(liubomir); 16t (Sofia Santos); 17b (Ok Nazarenko); 18tr (Jagodka);
15c (Waku); 19l & cover (Marilyn Volan); 20t (Fer Gregory); 20cr
(Stocksnapper); 21tl (Vezzani Photography); 21tr (Carolina K Smith
MD); 21br (Nicku); 22t (iDesign); 23t (Ralf Juergen Kraft); 23cl (Ian
Scott); 24bl (Poznyakov); 24br (Hunor Focze); 25tr (jannoon028); 25tl
(negative); 26t (YorkBerlin); 26b (Szocs Jozsef); 27t (Losevsky Photo
and Video); 29t (skyhawk); 29c (Cannaregio); 29b (Sarah Holmlund).
Wikipedia: 21cl (Luigi Chiesa); 28br. Cover images: fotofolia: lizard,
Einstein; iStockphoto.com: toast, plane, sky diver; Shutterstock.
com: earth, roller coaster

All other illustrations by Graham Rich

Every attempt has been made to clear copyright. Should there be any
inadvertent omission, please apply to the publisher for rectification.

Library and Archives Canada
Cataloguing in Publication

Claybourne, Anna
     Electric shocks and other energy evils / Anna Claybourne.

(Disgusting and dreadful science)
Includes index.
Issued also in electronic format.
ISBN 978-0-7787-0926-8 (bound).--ISBN 978-0-7787-0953-4 (pbk.)

     1. Electricity--Juvenile literature. I. Title. II. Series: Disgusting
and dreadful science

QC527.2.C54 2013   j537   C2012-907287-7

Library of Congress
Cataloging-in-Publication Data

CIP available at Library of Congress

Contents

ZZAPP!	4
World of wires	6
Electricity city	8
Power up!	10
Looping the loop	12
Shocking!	14
Dramatic static	16
Struck by lightning	18
Bright sparks	20
Electric life	22
Electric medicine	24
Frankenstein's monster	26
Into the future	28
Glossary	30
Websites and Places to visit	31
Index	32

ZZAPP!

CRACKLE! Yeeeouch! As you know, it's an incredibly bad idea to touch electric sockets, wiring, or the insides of electric gadgets or machines. That's because electricity can give you a painful shock. It can even be deadly.

ZAP CRACKLE YEEOUCH!

Ouch!

Electricity can flow through the human body, and this is why it can give us a shock. The stronger the current, and the longer it flows for, the more dangerous it is. Serious electric shocks can cause nasty burns, injuries, and worse!

Living dangerously

So why on EARTH do we have something as powerful and dangerous as electricity flowing around inside our houses? It's because electricity is so useful, it has become almost essential. We're so used to it, we'd be lost without it!

Electricity is power

Electricity is a type of energy, and that means it can do things for us. All sorts of things! Since we discovered how to use it, we've come up with millions of very useful inventions that run on its power, such as ovens, fridges, light bulbs, computers, traffic lights, microwaves, subway trains, radios... what else can you think of?

 ## See for Yourself

Life without electricity

Make a chart listing all the electrical appliances you use on a particular day – such as electric lights, alarm clock, electric toothbrush, fridge, kettle, TV, laptop, and so on. Then work out how you would do these jobs without electricity. Is there anything you really couldn't live without?

What is electricity made of?

Electricity comes in several forms and it can be hard to understand. Basically, it is a flow of particles, usually very small ones called **electrons**. Normally, electrons are not found on their own. They are tiny parts inside **atoms**, the building blocks that make up all the stuff around us.

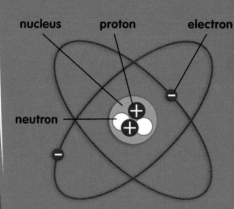

nucleus   proton   electron

neutron

Every atom is made up of a nucleus (packed with protons and neutrons) and electrons.

But in some substances, especially metals, electrons can break free, move around, and flow through a substance—something like water flowing in a river. A flow of electricity is called an **electric current**, and something that has electricity flowing through it, such as a wire, is described as **live**.

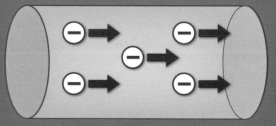

A live cable with electrons flowing through it

World of wires

Electricity is (almost) everywhere. It's in our homes, it powers streetlights, signs, trains, schools, and factories. All these things have to be connected by electrical wires, so that a supply of electricity can reach them.

Flow or no flow?

Only some materials, mainly metals, let electricity flow through them easily. They are called electrical **conductors**. Things that don't carry an electric current well are called **insulators**—like glass, rubber, and plastic. That's why many electric wires, such as the one at right, are made of a metal, such as copper, with a plastic covering for safety.

copper wires
(conductors)

plastic
coating
(insulators)

Transmission power

In most countries, there's a network or grid of big electrical cables criss-crossing the land. They carry electricity at a very high **voltage**, or energy level. These cables run to a substation where the voltage is lowered. Smaller power lines then carry lower voltage electricity into our homes and buildings. Inside our houses, wires carry electricity inside the walls to the electrical sockets.

Transmission towers are very hard to climb —for a good reason. If you did manage to get to the top of one, and touch a wire, the high voltage would frazzle you to a crisp!

Transmission towers carry electricity cables high above the ground.

Yuck!

In 1889, in the U.S.A., electricity worker John Feeks met a horrible death working on power lines on a busy street in New York. As he was electrocuted, it is reported that his body sizzled and burned while horrified people below could only watch. His body dangled there for a long while before the power was switched off and it was safe to get him down.

"I've saved a space for you, Blu. Just don't touch the tower"

So why don't birds fry!?

Birds sit on transmission towers and power cables and don't get hurt. That's because a bird doesn't give the electricity in the wire anywhere else to go. The electricity keeps going along the easiest path— the wire itself. However, if part of the bird also touched the tower, it would create an attractive path for the electricity, so it would flow through the bird and electrocute it.

Do not touch!

Transmission towers and their cables can stand up to most rain, wind, and snow storms, but there's one type of weather that can bring them down. In an ice storm, very cold rain falls and freezes onto every surface. Ice can build up on electricity cables, making them so heavy they snap. If you ever see one lying on the ground, **DO NOT TOUCH IT!** Call for help instead.

A severe ice storm in Canada in 1998 left people across Quebec without electricity for weeks.

Electricity city

Over the past 300 years, we've gone from having no electric machines to being surrounded by them. Setting up electricity supplies and cables is called electrification. It began in the UK and U.S.A. in the 1880s, and spread around the world. Today, every country has some kind of electricity supply, and in most places modern life depends on it.

We use electricity to heat water, cook, wash clothes, manage our money, learn, get around, light our homes, send messages, and have fun. Of course, all this means that if the electricity was suddenly switched off, we'd be a bit stuck. In fact, it does happen, and it's called a **blackout** or power outage.

Yuck!

One yucky effect of a blackout is fridges and freezers losing their power. All that food turns into a stinky, rotten mess.

DID YOU KNOW?

There are actually over a billion people in poorer parts of the world who do not have an electricity supply in their homes. But many of them still use electricity—at work or school, from batteries, or in wind-up electrical gadgets such as radios.

Blackout!

In 2003, a huge blackout hit the eastern U.S.A. and Canada when the electricity supply went wrong. It only lasted one night, but affected over 50 million people. Cities went dark, bank machines and tills closed down, trains stopped, and water cleaning systems failed, so people had to boil water to make it safe to drink.

On the plus side, everyone got a great view of the Milky Way (below), usually only seen from unpopulated places, such as Antarctica! Light from streets and buildings usually makes it very hard to see the stars clearly.

Rats have been the cause of some blackouts.

The computer age

Computers are one of the greatest electrical inventions of all. They contain tiny, very complicated electronic **circuits**. Electrical signals flowing around the circuits make the computer do all its calculations. This is how computers store facts, keep track of air traffic, access the Internet, and do all the other amazing jobs they do. Can you imagine life without them?

Over the years, we have invented smaller and smaller computer parts, and computers have shrunk and shrunk!

Computing in the 1950s

Computing as we know it today

Power up!

We know electricity passes along wires. But where do we get it from? Electricity is found in nature—lightning is a type of electricity, for example. However, lightning is too random to use as an energy supply. Instead, we have to generate electricity. For that, we can use all sorts of things, such as fuels like coal, gas and oil, underground heat, wind, water, and even poo!

Wind farms and solar panels harness natural energy from the wind and the Sun. Nuclear power stations make natural substances react in a way that produces huge amounts of energy.

Spinning wheels

To make electricity, energy is used to generate a spinning movement. For example, a river makes a waterwheel turn and wind makes a windmill spin round. Or with a fuel such as coal, power stations (such as the one left) use it to heat water and make steam, which spins a machine called a **turbine**. Another machine, called a **generator**, then turns the spinning motion into an electrical current. It does this by making a magnet spin around inside a coiled-up piece of wire, which creates an electrical charge.

Turn it off!

At the moment, we get a lot of our electricity by burning fossil fuels like coal and gas. There are two big problems with that! **One**: fossil fuels are eventually going to run out. **Two**: burning fuels makes air pollution, which leads to global warming. So it's important to save electricity and only use what you need.

Energy swap

Electricity is a type of energy. You can't make energy out of nothing. You can only turn one form of energy into another. To get electricity, you have to use another form of energy, such as the flow of wind, solar energy from the Sun, or the chemical energy stored in coal.

Yuck!

Some electricity really does come from poo. Zoos sometimes collect poo from elephants and other animals, then store it in big tanks. It rots and gives off a type of smelly gas called methane. The gas is collected and used as a fuel to generate electricity. This system can be used for people's homes, too—but it does need a LOT of poo!

You're doing WHAT with my poo....?

Chicken power!

Clever chicken farmers are turning the mountains of poo their chickens produce into electricity. In turn, the electricity is used to power the buildings, making the farms self-sufficient. Now that's poultry power!

11

Looping the loop

To keep working, electricity has to flow around in a loop called a circuit. Its power comes from the flow of electrons pushing along a wire or cable – just as a river makes a waterwheel work, or wind blows a windmill.

A simple circuit

All a circuit needs is a power source, such as a battery, and wires to carry the electricity around the circuit. You can add a bulb and a switch to really see what's going on!

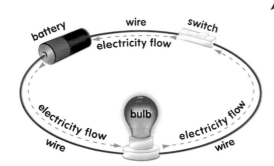

battery
wire
switch
electricity flow
electricity flow
bulb
electricity flow
wire
wire

If the switch is on, the bulb will glow because the electricity is flowing from one end of the battery, round the loop, to the other end. If the switch is off, the circuit is broken and the electricity doesn't flow.

Circuit diagrams

A circuit diagram shows the parts of a circuit clearly and simply. Lines show the wires and symbols are used to represent the other **components** (bits and pieces). Here's the simple circuit above drawn as a diagram.

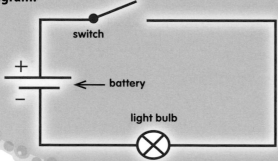

switch
+
−
battery
light bulb

⊗ **Light bulb** A light bulb glows when electricity flows through it.

⌐⌐ **Switch** The switch is a break in the circuit. When you close it, the circuit joins together and electricity can flow.

⊣⊢ **Battery** A battery or another type of energy cell provides the electrical charge.

Ⓜ **Motor** A **motor** uses a flow of electricity to make a rotating motion. Motors are used in fans, CD drives, toys, and any gadget that makes something spin or turn.

This is a key, or legend, to some of the most common components used in circuit diagrams.

Some batteries contain very strong acids or other chemicals. That's why they're packed inside a tough case. If they leak, the chemicals can get out and burn your clothes or skin.

Where's it coming from?

In our circuit, the electricity is coming from the battery. Batteries are very useful for small, low-energy, portable gadgets like flashlights and phones. They turn energy from chemicals into electrical charge, which pulls on electrons and makes them move. Electrons flow from one end, or **terminal** of a battery around the circuit to the other end. The sockets in our homes work the same way. When a gadget is plugged into a socket, it's connected to the electricity supply, making a loop that electricity flows around.

See for Yourself

Build a circuit

You could try building a circuit like the one opposite using wires and components from an electronics or hardware store. Get an adult to help you.

What do circuits look like?

Real circuits inside computers and other gadgets are often complicated, and might look a bit like those above. The wires and other components are tiny and hard to see.

shocking!

Getting an electric shock is horrible! Even a weak one can hurt and make you feel trembly, sweaty, and scared. Stronger shocks can kill you. **Yikes!**

What does it do?

Our bodies actually use electricity to work (see page 22). Muscles spring into action when they receive a tiny electrical signal from the brain. So if a lot of electricity floods through your whole body, it can make all your muscles jump, jerk, and go berserk. That includes your heart muscles. This means a big electric shock can make your heart stop working. Being killed by electricity is called **electrocution**.

Shock safety

There's plenty you can do to make sure you DON'T get an electric shock.

Zapped!

A bug zapper uses a blue light to attract flies and other buzzing pests. It then electrocutes them when they touch a grid of live wires. The dead flies fall down and collect in a tray at the bottom.

Nice!

- *Never touch electrical equipment with wet hands.*
- *Never use an electrical device that has a frayed or damaged cord or plug.*
- *Don't take electrical equipment apart.*
- *A sign like the one above means powerful electricity is being used. Stay away!*

Shocked on purpose!

The zapping power of electricity can be used against people, and sometimes animals, too. Here are a few shocking inventions:

• **Electric fence** (right)– a wire fence with electricity running through it. It keeps animals in (such as this sad bear) and trespassers out!

• **Cattle prod** – a stick used to give farm animals a small, unpleasant electric shock to get them moving. Some people think these are cruel and should be banned.

• **Electroshock weapon** (below) – this shoots out darts that cause an electric shock and stop the muscles from working. It can be used to control or catch suspected criminals.

• **Electric chair** – the scariest of all! This method of execution kills its victim by electrocution.

I just want to be free...

This electroshock weapon is a TASER®, popular with police forces around the world. Here, the cartridge has been removed at the front, revealing the arc of electricity.

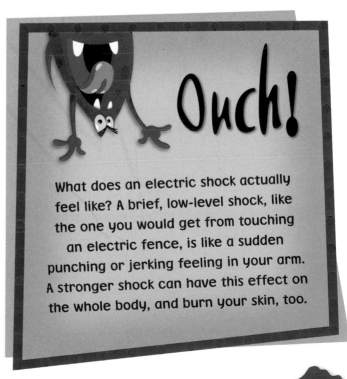

Ouch!

What does an electric shock actually feel like? A brief, low-level shock, like the one you would get from touching an electric fence, is like a sudden punching or jerking feeling in your arm. A stronger shock can have this effect on the whole body, and burn your skin, too.

15

Dramatic static

More than 2,000 years ago, an ancient Greek named Thales found that rubbing a piece of amber with cat fur seemed to make it "sticky"—it pulled small objects toward it. He had discovered static electricity, which can collect in one place, jump, and spark, instead of flow like normal electricity.

Yeeouch, get away with that!

Amber is fossilized tree sap that makes a good electrical insulator.

No flow

Have you ever felt your hair crackle when you pull a sweater over your head or when you comb your hair? This is **static electricity**. It is an electrical charge that doesn't flow through a wire or other substances. When you comb your hair, electrons rub off onto the comb and it becomes charged. But plastic is an insulator – it can't carry electricity away. Instead, the charge builds up on its surface.

Sticky static

Electrons have a negative or "minus" (-) charge, so they are drawn toward anything with a positive (+) charge. If you charge a comb or a balloon with static electricity, it will become "sticky," and draw things to it like a magnet.

16

Ouch!

In the 1700s, scientists invented the Leyden jar, a machine for storing a large amount of static charge. In one experiment, they sent a painful static spark from a Leyden jar though a chain of 180 French palace guards all holding hands in a row (right).

Don't worry, chaps. This won't hurt a bit.

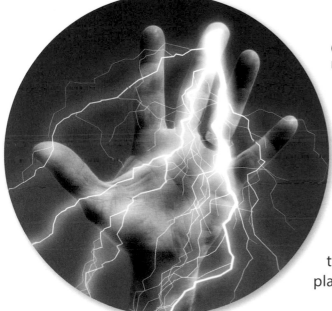

Shocking static

Touching a shopping cart or car door can give you a "static shock." Sometimes you even hear a little zapping sound. What's going on? The cart has built up a static charge from rubbing on things. It can't flow away because the cart's rubbery wheels are insulators. When you touch the cart with your finger, electrons jump across the gap, to let the charge escape. Static can build up in your body in the same way, especially if your shoes have rubber or plastic soles.

See for Yourself

Hair-raising test

Blow up a balloon and tie it. Rub it against your hair for a few seconds. Then lift up the balloon. The rubbing has transferred electrons from your hair to the balloon, giving it a static charge, and it pulls your hair up in the air! *(This works best on fine, straight hair —if yours doesn't work, try a friend's!)*

Struck by lightning

A shock from an electric socket can be pretty nasty. So imagine being hit by an electrical bolt from the sky, thousands of times more powerful than that, and hotter than the surface of the Sun! Lightning strikes are VERY dangerous—often deadly. However, many people have survived them.

What is lightning?

In ancient times, people thought the gods threw lightning strikes, or "thunderbolts," down from the sky to zap anyone who had annoyed them. But now we know more about what really causes lightning.

It happens during thunderstorms, when the undersides of clouds gather a strong negative static charge, while the ground has a positive charge. Eventually, a huge spark jumps across the gap to balance out the opposite charges. It's similar to getting a static electric shock from a shopping cart, but on a much bigger scale.

DID YOU KNOW?

There's another kind of lightning, too. It's weird, spooky "ball lightning." It's very rare and scientists aren't sure what causes it. It can appear during a thunderstorm as a glowing, floating ball that passes through walls and windows. It has been known to burn and sometimes kill people.

HOW hot???

This may look like a tree stump (above), but it is called a fulgurite and it's made of glass. It was formed when a blast of lightning hit a sandy beach or desert and traveled in different directions. A lightning strike can not only melt sand. It can heat the air around it to 36,032°F (20,000°C)—that's around four times hotter than the Sun's surface. It makes the air expand suddenly, creating the sound wave that we hear as thunder.

Ouch!

American park ranger Roy Sullivan was the most struck-by-lightning person in history. He survived an amazing seven separate lightning strikes! He had his toes, legs, stomach, and eyebrows burned, and his hair was set on fire several times.

Saved by my rubber boots!

Sometimes, wearing rubber boots has helped lightning victims survive. The rubbery boots are insulators and resist the flow of electricity, so they stop the lightning from flowing right through the body.

Bright sparks

These bright sparks of science led the way to the electric world we have today...

Franklin's electric fire

In the 1750s, American scientist Benjamin Franklin showed that lightning was electric. His experiment involved flying a kite in a thunderstorm, with a key at the bottom of the kite string. Electric charge from the clouds gathered in the kite, flowed along the wet kite string, and made sparks fly out of the key. Franklin also invented the lightning conductor—a metal wire leading from the top of a tall building to the ground, to carry lightning strikes safely away.

Would a scientist as clever as me really be THAT silly?

SAFETY WARNING!

Franklin wrote about his lightning experiment, but no one knows if he actually did it himself. If he did, he was VERY FOOLISH! Flying a kite in a thunderstorm is an incredibly bad idea. Several other people died from lightning strikes while trying it out.

Jumping frogs' legs!

Gulp!

In 1781, Italian scientist Luigi Galvani was experimenting with frogs' legs. His steel knife touched a frog's leg and a brass hook it was fixed to. The leg jumped by itself! Galvani thought the leg must contain some kind of electrical liquid to make it move. But another scientist, Alessandro Volta, saw something else in Galvani's work...

Volta's pile

zinc
copper
salty disk

Volta realized that the frog's leg itself wasn't producing electricity. Instead, something was enabling electricity to flow through it. Volta found that connecting two different metals with salty liquid between them (like Galvani's knife, hook, and frog) could make an electric current flow. In 1800, he built a pile of copper, zinc, and damp, salty cloth disks, and attached it to a wire circuit. Electricity flowed! Volta's invention, called the voltaic pile, was the first battery.

Faraday's inventions

In 1821, British scientist Michael Faraday found out how to use electricity to make a magnet move. Then he discovered the reverse effect—using a moving magnet to make an electric current. His work paved the way for the modern motors and generators we now use every day.

Electric life

T hink of an electrical machine, and you'll probably think of a computer, TV, or phone. But you yourself are an electrical machine, too—one of the most complicated there is!

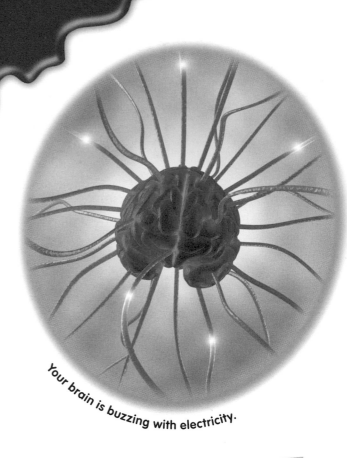

Your brain is buzzing with electricity.

Signaling system

Your body uses electricity to carry information around, as part of the nervous system. Electrical signals travel along nerve cells from your senses to your brain, to tell it what you can see, hear, and so on. In your brain, thinking and remembering happens when electricity zooms along nerve cell branches. And to make you move, your brain sends electrical signals to your muscles.

Electricity rushes around your body along your nerves (yellow in this picture).

Ouch!

Some animals, like electric eels and rays, use electricity as a weapon to stun prey or fight off predators. After the explorer Alexander von Humboldt was zapped by an electric eel on his travels in South America, he said, "I do not remember having ever received...a more dreadful shock...I was affected during the rest of the day with a violent pain in the knees, and in almost every joint."

Remote-controlled bull

Hey! Why can't I move?

In 1965, U.S. scientist Jose Delgado invented the stimoceiver, a machine that can send electrical signals into human and animal brains. In tests, it made volunteers experience strange feelings and move their limbs against their will. He also used a stimoceiver to control an angry bull, and make it stop charging toward him!

DID YOU KNOW?

Sharks don't just see or sniff out their prey – they have an amazing electrical sixth sense. They can detect the electricity in other animals' bodies, using little pit-shaped organs on their snouts.

 ## See for Yourself

Test your reflexes

Cross your legs with one knee on top of the other, then tap just below your kneecap with the edge of a book. If you hit the right spot, your knee will kick! Electrical signals zoom to and from your spine, and you react almost at once, without thinking.

Electric medicine

Electric shocks aren't just painful accidents or horrible methods of punishment. They have all kinds of useful effects, too, especially if you're ill. In Victorian times, people believed electricity was a great health treatment, and lined up to get electric shocks. Today, we still use it, as it's been shown to work for all kinds of things.

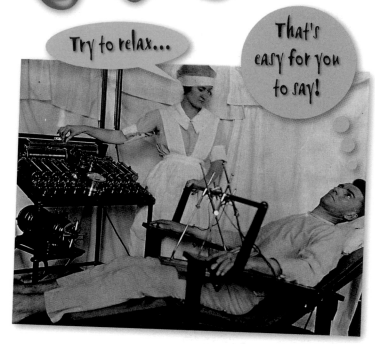

Try to relax...

That's easy for you to say!

Mind shock

A powerful electric shock to the brain sounds nasty, but this treatment is still used to treat some kinds of mental illness. For some people, it works when nothing else does. It can look scary though, as the shock makes the patient jerk and wriggle around.

Blip! Blip!

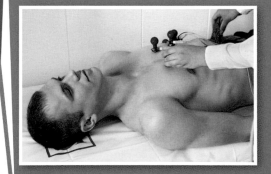

Like other muscles, your heart is controlled by electricity. An ECG (electrocardiogram) machine can detect this electrical activity, and show your heartbeat on a screen. A similar device can read your brain's electrical patterns, or brainwaves. Doctors use these to check for heart and brain problems.

Heart attack

When someone is having a heart attack, doctors and paramedics can use defibrillator paddles to give the heart a quick electric shock. This electrical energy can regulate dangerously high or low heartbeats or even reactivate a stopped heart.

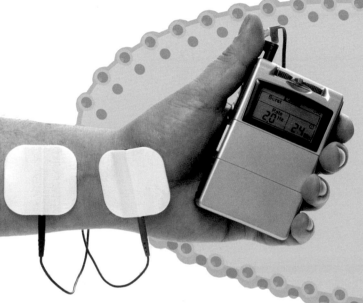

Stop the pain!

Electricity can even be a painkiller! TENS machines zap nerves in your skin with a mild electrical current. This bombards the brain with a non-painful sensation, which gets in the way of pain signals. It can also make the body release its own painkillers.

Yikes!

Many astronauts need gentle electric therapy on their muscles when they return from space because their muscles have started to waste away from lack of use!

NASA astronaut Tracy Caldwell Dyson and fellow Russian cosmonaut just after returning to Earth following six months on the International Space Station.

Frankenstein's monster

In Mary Shelley's famous book, Dr. Frankenstein creates a monstrous creature from body parts, and uses electricity to give it "a spark of being", and bring it to life. But could this really happen some time in the future?

Zapping the dead

Frankenstein was written in 1818, when experiments with electricity were big news. Scientists really did try to bring dead people back to life with electric shocks, giving Shelley the idea for her story. This was named Galvanism, after the famous frog experimenter, Luigi Galvani (page 21).

In other experiments, scientists also made dead bodies sit up, groan, and thrash around. However, they hadn't really come back to life. Just like Galvani's frog's leg, their muscles moved when the electricity ran through them—but they weren't alive, awake, or in control at all.

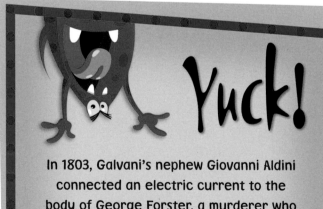

Yuck!

In 1803, Galvani's nephew Giovanni Aldini connected an electric current to the body of George Forster, a murderer who had just been executed. As he expected, the body began to move...

"...the jaws of the deceased criminal began to quiver, and the adjoining muscles were horribly contorted, and one eye was actually opened...The right hand was raised and clenched, and the legs and thighs were set in motion."

Clones

However, we do sometimes use electricity to create life, as part of the process of **cloning**. Cloning means making an exact copy of a living thing. Dolly the sheep was the first animal to be cloned successfully in 1996. Since then other sheep, cats, and many other animals have been cloned. To do it, scientists have to take a cell from one animal, and combine it with an egg cell from another. When the new cell is ready, a small jolt of electricity makes it start working and growing.

Cloning human babies is banned in most countries – although it is possible. Can you imagine having a clone? But even though you would be exactly the same genetically, your minds would be unique and different experiences growing up would shape your characters.

Model armies

Clones are often featured in scary sci-fi stories. Could armies of identical human clones really take over the world? Well, only if their brains were manipulated or replaced, making them behave like obedient robots.

Into the future

Thanks to electricity, a lot of "futuristic" things are already here! We have videophones, robots, voice-activated computers, and many other gadgets first seen in sci-fi films. What's coming next?

Ouch!

We might opt to have microchips implanted into our brains to give us instant information from the Internet!

Inventions galore

Electricity can power just about any machine, so inventors keep on coming up with new gadgets. They're developing electronic paper, flying cars, mind-controlled machines, invisibility devices, and technology that can turn any screen or surface into a computer keyboard—even your hand or arm!

People power

You could even become a walking, talking electricity supply yourself. Solar backpacks (right) have solar panels that generate electricity from sunlight, so you can plug in your laptop, tablet, or phone when you're out and about! Scientists are also working on ways to power small devices from your own body heat.

Bionic body parts

Many people are alive today thanks to a little electrical device connected to their heart called a pacemaker (right). But now the first completely artificial electric hearts are here, too. New electronic ears, eyes, and limbs are being tested and, in the future, these inventions will get better. Who knows what bionic body parts will be invented next?

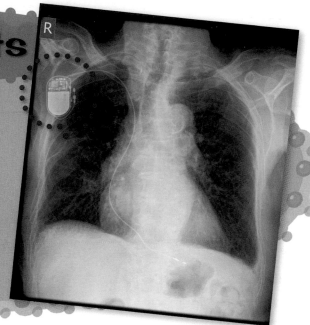

A model solar-powered car

Electric planet

Most of the world's population is now dependent on electricity. We are using up all our planet's fossil fuels to generate it, but soon they will run out. What then? We need to find new ways to get electricity. In the future, we'll probably rely much more on solar power from the Sun, wind, and wave and tidal energy. Many machines, from phones to cars, could run on electricity from their own solar panels.

In some ways, computers are very much like human brains, with electrical signals whizzing around a huge network of wires.

Artificial intelligence

Scientists working on artificial intelligence are creating computers that can make decisions, learn from experience, and have life-like conversations. Meanwhile, robot designers are building more and more realistic, advanced robots that can sense their surroundings and move like real living things. By combining these two things, we could create proper walking, talking human or animal robots, just like in films.

Glossary

atoms Tiny units that all materials are made of

blackout A failure of the electricity supply

circuit A loop that electricity can flow around

cloning Making exact copies of living things

components The working parts of an electric circuit

conductor A material that can carry a flow of electricity

electric current A flow of electricity through a substance

electrocution Being killed by an electric shock

electron A tiny particle that makes up part of an atom

generator A device that converts a spinning movement into a flow of electricity

insulator A material that does not carry a flow of electricity easily

live Carrying an electric current

motor A device that converts electricity into a rotating movement

solar panel A flat sheet of a material that collects sunlight and converts it into a flow of electricity

static electricity Electricity that builds up in one place instead of flowing

terminal One of the ends or attachment points of a battery

turbine A device that converts other forms of energy, such as wind or steam power, into a spinning movement

voltage The force, measured in volts, of an electrical current

Websites and Places to visit

www.think-energy.co.uk
Jam-packed with energy-related activities and information, split into four age groups, from 7 to 18 years.

www.electrocity.co.nz
ElectroCity is a fun SIMS-style game from New Zealand, which lets you build and manage your own virtual town or city, learning about energy and sustainability along the way.

www.energyhog.org/childrens.htm
Funny games showing you ways to improve the energy efficiency of your home.

http://energyquest.ca.gov/story/index.html
A Californian site with games, movies, and information.

www.eia.gov/kids/
This site is packed with lots of information about energy and electricity, as well as games and activities.

www.pbs.org/benfranklin/exp_shocking.html
An interactive exploration of the experiments that led to Ben Franklin's discovery of electricity.

SPARK Museum of Electrical Invention
1213 Bay Street
Bellingham, Washington 98225 U.S.A.
www.sparkmuseum.org/

The Electricity Gallery @ MOSI
Museum of Science and Industry
Liverpool Road, Castlefield,
Manchester M3 4FP, UK
www.mosi.org.uk

Ontario Science Centre
770 Don Mills Road
Toronto, Ontario M3C 1T3
Canada
www.ontariosciencecentre.ca/

Magna Science Adventure Centre
Sheffield Road, Templeborough,
Rotherham S60 1DX, UK
www.visitmagna.co.uk

Smithsonian National Air and Space Museum
National Mall Building:
Independence Avenue at 6th Street,
SW Washington, DC 20560, U.S.A.
www.nasm.si.edu

Steven F. Udvar-Hazy Center:
14390 Air and Space Museum
Parkway, Chantilly, VA 20151, U.S.A.

Index

Aldini, Giovanni 26
amber 16
astronauts 25
atoms 5
batteries 8, 12, 13, 21
birds 7
blackouts 8, 9
cables 5, 6-7, 12
Caldwell Dyson, Tracy 25
cattle prod 15
circuit diagram 12
circuits 9, 12-13, 21
clones 27
coal 10, 11
components 12, 13
computers 5, 9, 13, 22, 28, 29
conductors 6, 20
Delgado, Jose 23
Dolly the sheep 27
electric chair 15
electric charge 10, 12, 13, 16, 17, 18, 20
electric current 4, 5, 6, 10, 21, 25, 26
electric eels 22
electric fence 15
electric shock 4, 14-17, 18, 22, 24-25, 26
electric sockets 4, 6, 13, 16, 18
electrical appliances/ gadgets 4, 5, 8, 12, 13, 28

electricity
    what it's made of 5
    where it comes from 10-11
electrification 8-9
electrocardiogram (ECG) 24
electrons 5, 12, 13, 16, 17
energy 5, 6, 10-11, 13, 25, 29
experiments
    Build a circuit 13
    Hair-raising test 17
    Life without electricity 5
    Test your reflexes 23
Faraday, Michael 21
Feeks, John 7
Forster, George 26
fossil fuels 10, 29
Frankenstein 26
Franklin, Benjamin 20
fulgurite 17
Galvani, Luigi 21, 26
Galvanism 26
gas 10, 11
generator 10
global warming 10
heart 14, 24, 25, 29
human body 4, 14, 22-27
ice storm 7
insulators 6, 17, 18, 19
Leyden jar 17
lightning 10, 18-19, 20
muscles 14, 15, 22, 24, 25,26

nerves 22, 25
nuclear power 10
outage see blackouts
pollution 10
poo (as fuel) 10-11
robots 27, 29
rubber insulators 6, 17, 19
sharks 23
Shelley, Mary 26
solar energy 10, 11, 29
solar panels 10, 28, 29
static electricity 16-17, 18
stimoceiver 23
Sullivan, Roy 19
TASER® 15
TENS machine 25
Thales 18
transmission towers 6-7
turbine 10
Volta, Alessandro 21
voltage 6
voltaic pile 21
von Humboldt, Alexander 22
wave and tidal energy 29
wind power 10, 11, 12, 29